THE
FACE LOOKING
COMPANY

THE BEGINNING LOVE WALK AROUND THE WORLD

Robert Martin

authorHOUSE®

AuthorHouse™
1663 Liberty Drive
Bloomington, IN 47403
www.authorhouse.com
Phone: 1 (800) 839-8640

Published by AuthorHouse 08/02/2017

ISBN: 978-1-5246-2631-0 (sc)
ISBN: 978-1-5246-2630-3 (hc)
ISBN: 978-1-5246-2629-7 (e)

Library of Congress Control Number: 2017911867

Print information available on the last page.

Hey are Hello

First do not look over this letter, that we are sending to you. My name is Robert Lee Martin and we are looking for some very very good information, from IBM. You built a computer that will smell and tell the doctor about people and touch hear see taste in 5 years sense or smell are in the computer data base or in the cognitive computer search as Waston that is playing and talking on TV. You IBM have to talk to me about my part in the cognitive computer world. I have a provisional application for patent and a non-provisional (utility) patent application filing with and filer authorized by: Attorney Docket Number and name Luca Dotton 2012IDSRM1P power of attorney 56341 we do not no what the power of attorney is up to. He do not get in contact, with us no more, to give us 1 utility provisional patent number to the cognitive computer we are look for IBM to contact us at this phone number 601-807-0628 are sweetroo8@ yahoo.com This agreement, dated as of the date set forth herein, is between IBM non-disclosure and confidentiality agreement This is what we are talk about getting performances contemplated

hereby shall be governed and construed under and according to the law of the state of <u>my address</u> 3995 McClain Road Liberty, Miss 39645. Help identify my new smell and tell 1st named Inventor/ Applicant Name: Robert L. Martin

Author: Of Cognitive of thing that tell you about IBM ins 2012???

Built to go in rubber and hole your dick in the rubber holder and you pee in the rubber holder and it go down the pipe into the pee bag. When you get in a place you can open the unlock plug from the bag, and the pee will come out on the ground and not on your foot. This is new for men that pee on themself. No more peeing on themself.

A rubber cup to put his dick in it at all time if he want to you can hook on to his anusal if need.

Pipe

Bag

A Bag will go around your legs under your pants that come from your pen

Hook and unhook from his leg

A cup that come from a man pen and run down his legs and he pee in the plastic bag, and when he pee in the bag and on the side of the bag he can pour out the pee that he put in the pee bag

A pee bag on the side of my legs to catch my pee so I will not pee on myself no more.

This is a pee bag keep your close dry no more pee in your peant

My name is Robert T. Martin Hello to the Library of Congress Thank for everything I can not stop writing. I claim this idea are invention. What idea are we talking about? The house that I live in, yes my house what about that house you live in I am talking about the windows in my house. I did not invent the windows I did not say I invent the windows. I am trying to put a see through tent in my windows, a tent that go on your house windows, this is a special kind of tent. Tent that no one can see in my house, but I can see out side at night and see who are at my house at night. I am taking the night vision house windows to be built for house and car night vision windows if I can put this on cars. This is new for a house, my house need this night vision in my windows. The night vision is a tent like day, you can see at night like day. That the house windows tent I will put in my windows at night in my house when I look outside I see day through the night vision windows, tent. That come from night vision.

D and A Lock and unlock thing

Robert Love Money

Logo

Every thing move
In the world
The book that no one, wont
to read warning this book may
not be for your mind.

Why?

Because I never heard the preachers say God teacher me how to go to heaven and when I get me how to stay in heaven after we get to heaven. We know that the men teachers the book of the Bible the Holy Bible but I think we have to learn God way by asking for the way he know about all. We don't want to be kick out of heaven please keep me in the right pass to the heavenly air.

God teaches me how to get to heaven and to keep me in heaven when I get there. The Face Looking Company my logo say the bible love walk around the world only one time the Face Looking Company face to face looking for time bone recording one mud bone why? He is making all recording of the world w-h-y why heaven your

So I am time I say we me me of we we me me

who is (I NOT) I not did I not die? (I not die) Yes I not die and went to see the dream of the mind. Who is (I NOT)? I have a I, but where are the not. The trees has not on them. We say we got the good out of trees, yes because we eat from them, some of them, so this computer that smell and tell you all kind of thing, Robert Martin has my five senses of the words remeble so my computer smell and tell has are have it's senses of the new world order for doctor to know about people sicken and this computer know about the D and A of people. The computer talk to people.

God teaches me that heaven and hell is on earth. Heaven and hell is in me. Heaven and hell is in the mind.

1. Lucifer was kicked out for starting trouble.
2. You stay in me or by
3. Write about the medical side.

The book that no one want to read. The why go on the back are the book. One word on the back side the word is why

I like to say we discover a clue. But I have to say I discover me and other, what did he say? He mean other, discover him first, they would say they did. But this is what I find about writing are art are visual detection visualize or visualized. I find or found the way some thing work, what do you mean how thing work, for you or for me. For me I am talking about people and the discover or me. I do not know what your saying about people I am saying dead people to me say thing in there on way, to the believe of me I hear the row are the win, and the voice are people in the win, when it blow around my house. When I see myself living around some are thing that hear and say thing I am saying thing about me, also and living people I think the dead all ways wont to come back throw the win the storm throw any way they can. I thank they are mad, with who? There self of other. Who to say,

This Reading May Boggle your Mind

The dead show that live the liven say what did you bring me, a dream what was in that dream? You living who are living the dead? O you are living in me what did you bring me in that dream food are word of through I ask where are you and who are you in my dream life, are you the mirror. You are we; are we we the people that live and die. Are you mother nature that repelled and recycle or redo the world at all time. World recycling itself with the help of God. The world is doing a good job. The world has a job to stay clean and smell clean. Who are my dream life, that's me me that the name I said. For the way he know about all. Warning this book may be for your mind because this is not the bible, this book is about the title to a lot or thing that the mind are looking for the good out of trees and good out of man. But this warning might not befor your mind or this reading my call you to get confuse. Then you may be confuse already.

What about me? Yes I put a lot of thing together

in my years. Like what! All that people know about idea and invention about the air bag suite we have put around people for the safe, are working, we are talking years ago. Why are we talking about old news to tell you about the new ways or the book that you will know about the invention. How mennonite you will talk about? If I can put all are them in the book I will say something about the computer smell and tell. This is the one that no one wont to let you know about, because it will know everything about me and other people die are live. They like to play with me but this is no game this is the true and nothing but the true so see yourself when you walk through the one that tell, all about people. But you say, well: there are no markets for people that live the true. If we built the true of the world can you handled. The device that no you, and me at all time. So I do not like to tell about people sometime. Why not? Because they try to take my device one piece at a time, and put it on something, and call, something that is third. I am the author are the world of man and woman that live with this computer that live the true and tell the true walk though are in the camera and it

tell you name and your D and A your height your weight san your body smell your body tell on you what you do at any time you need to know. Man want to keep gun in there life. But change is coming one day can you see? Mc in some of the safe proof shoes when I am walking in the wood and I do not have the safe proof shoe on my feet. A stick can go through your feet are a nail when you or who every on the outside working. We are read people with the sniffing sensor to get it right. Do you think people are unread in the world? Watching you, do thing as we look for other to teach the people are learning right of other. Right are the way I smell, I awful stink are smell bad that is your right to smell horrible are smell to a good? Taste, my sniffing sensor are looking for the smell of all thing that can go in the computer. It's too good to be what it is, but we say good come from all people some time. We have a belt that will spray off around your body, to kill West Nile mosquito are help keep the mosquito from being around you or biting you, the timer spray belt automatic response or hat. Hey how does. I response to people that never been discover.

Where are other people in the world that we do not know about. I can only tell you about me. I am fifty three years old and I can tell you about some of the other in the world are in my dream. People come and go through my mind. When I thank that I am asleep hoping this is true that came in my mind, a dream about other people. Think are people only when I am asleep who are those people? They do not come in my mind in the day time, like they come at night. What are they bring me, good will good luck a gold are this unread from the mind are from the people that be on your mind are in your dream. I do not has to say what other people say, they say, they seen in there mind I know when its in my mine and leave me with no good understand about the ways it subscribers. The notice we received from the dream is this the same as the win of the rowing that we hear in the day time win are night time win. We ask Menny? To governing the sale of the computer smell and tell to keep the world safe with this invention I heard, in my life if wall can talk, they will tell on you. When I am inside my house how do they come in my house and talk to me, is

my wall talking to me, and other men and woman in the dream of life. To make this clear you has to know yourself to understand what you know in the life are sleep and dreaming. To understand me and check the through that you think you know what they say, when you are in that bed or dream. Am I the same dream that come and go through my mind I think not why? Do the dream worry you. Is this the way this suppose to be with people over the years that we pass though the earth of air. We use air for a lot are thing I can never tell you all the thing that air are use for. Air is the most thing we use in the world, are we can call it the win do you think the dream that come in my mind is air? Are what? The book that no one know the calls for insistently the demands come over you. And we we eyes can not see it. Only can hear it in the dream and her ear splitting and my noisy in my ear. Have you ever has a man or a woman licks there tongue out at you and you did not say nothing are did not lick your tongue out at them. Why did that happy and I did nothing but look at the people lick their tunnel out and I move on.

When people speak to me some time they say, what up man, I say you are standing up and life is good for you and me. And he will say yes life is good. How do you know life is good, I say you are living and breather the air of the world, I said this is some are the best thing to happy to mankind, do you think, He leave and say no more at that time. I go on and keep trying to discover the ear plug. Do you think the ear plug will stop the dream that come in my ear are my mind which one come first. When you turn the radio on and put the ear plug in your ear the dream life no longer come in your mind. Is this my body come out, my body and come back in my dick when they get ready to come back in my mind are body. It seem like I am not one body. As my mind travel through my soul I offing think about the down side or my body, you lay down one time a night. If you do not have to go to the bathroom. But I look on the upper side of my soul are mind are body, what do you see? I see the up side of my life, I wake up I get up I stand up and I prop up. Do you think that this device is professor's protection, that talk to the skill that we need to know about to promoted me

to a higher position, will I every benefit or gain or produce the print that was in my body. We have print, or handprint on the computer smell and tell. This project can help see the proof of a crime. Property that is not your claim put it back it seen like some come and go in there mind the prospect for the outlook in mind. Is this just a try out or just the future of the way or succeeds. We think are I think when I go to the bathroom and lost my waste. Do you put baby back in your body are dream back in your body, we know we put food back into your body, to make age. How old the days is? Are the night older than the days? Do the night have waste? Do the days have waste are the world older than the night and the days. I think the earth is younger than the world. What does the earth do with it waste? What does the world do with its waste. I like to give the world his social security number. I am stand up and the sun go over me in the day time. Until night time and then the door close for the sun and the door open for the night to come out. I am reading my mind, are the world reading my mind in the word. So I said hear the heaven out the word earth. Just a trough. When

people read this book do not thank about just you, thank about all the love you are around. Just some are the thing to talk about, the love of money the love or love, love to speak love to work love to have thing the love of kids I can go on and on naming the way love is around us, and in us. The food or love, I like to say this if I made love to a lady, and she get baby during that time, and the man do not know that she are with his baby, because she will not tell him another about the baby, maybe I may have kids in the world that I do not know about, repelled back and see. See when I look out in to the world and see something that I see, are never seen in my life time. A man that look like the world. I have some part are the world like air and we grow up like a tree you understand this part about me. But I am talking about a man looking like the world. Can you look like the world? The man that I was looking for that looking like the world do he have the mouth of the ground, the way that ground open up and eat thing that around it. This man is all in one, the mouth or the man and the tree or the man, the stop sign or the man the road of the man the house of the man the store of the man the car

of the man water of the man the everything of the man, we built the man out of everything we can think of. And we made one man just that big. How big is this man, that I never seen. How deep is the earth. How long is the earth. How big is the world. I was trying to built the biggest man in the world out or thing in the world. Repelled back I though about reverse, for one, what? I said for one dog. Can be so big, I spell dog backer and it spell God. If I do not take a bath I will stink, where dose all the stink go from the world. The world smell so good to me, and so fresh. This book may not be a good book for you to read. It may be the power over your mind and you can handly the way the thing do in this world. You can get out the heat just go in the cool air, air that man made cool. We will still read the people in this world, every day, with the telling device there everything that need to be read about one and tell it on them. Why because you can get it right. Some of it can be made right. The man can control some are the air, but he cannot control the air he breath, and you can rule sometime but not all the time.

Do you think everything in the world move in some way of other? Do the world pastor it on funeral when a tree die of a cow die are grass die or what every die in the world. So do you think the world is good to itself, how can you tell? Its not bad. Some will say its a good day are a bad day on earth. What about in the heaven around the star is good because I never heard no one say that, bad was around the star and in the heaven. The voice recognized that the ford are who so every has it is wrong. Because the letter that set in the Library of Congress copyright to the computer smell and tell you, who you are. I am the first man to tell the identified of all people over the whole world. Identification label name tag. I think I need to sue the one that take from identification of mankind that is already, have you in the computer that label you. The authors are your everything my voice is Robert Martin who on the right to the identification or all people. Only your picture and your address and my voice and your D and A just to keep you safe and keep you in the right. Of the smell and tell, only hole your database for the law man if need.

When I spoke to the copyright about tell the thing that I know on all people and a lot are thing. When I speak the word to the invention you know who I am. Will my computer smell and tell you and me about people that walk around the world. I like to see you put your voice in the ghost house and tell me who are the people name in that ghost house. But we are not really looking into you lie. You should turn the identification for all people back to the computer smell and tell. See when I tell you my idea about thing in the world, you will try to use it your way, and make my ideas not know. Paten retail are whatever the company it may be, it tell you one thing and tell me another thing about my invention. You tell me there are no market place for the computer smell and tell identification of all people label. I am going to tell you some more about my knowledge so you can try to change are get around it so you think you can thank for me but cannot. This is some are the dream that come at night. To know what that dream tell me is a good thing. Here is what I tell from my mind, we talk about a number for the world. In mine I own the world, smart device.

And here are the address and zip code to the world, I did not say the earth I on, but I am walk on the earth. Do not say that I am playing with the heaven maybe you need some of this information on an up and up instance. So to get where you are going in the world. You say you went to the moon I did not ask for the address of no number to the moon. I just ask about worlds are the heaven number, of storm. Go across the earth and you track them and give them names but I never hear you give them a address or a zip code, when the storm stop. And another start, so storm has went through many of town and city that have zip code and address, so the storm use all of the zip code and address it need. Do the world have a voice? It the voice of many thing gravity march the sky we are not ask you to give me the number to everything that in the sky, we ask for one SS number, the world, do we need it? If we need immediate what would we do. This is not talk about the bible This is talk about we, who are we, to come in the world are earth and leave out this place

The face looking company the dream of a lot of

people the face looking for time bone you know, you look in the mirror and you see WeWe in that mirror who did you see WeWe in your mirror It have to be you. We stay for a later time here on earth, and we go to time bone and wait for our time. To face the time turning thought the world or through earth its call what? The way it is, we look at faces every day, and some at night in that dream. Is that me in my dream dead are my real dead, facing something in a life turning to see you. Facing the fact in the life of standing this is not bad, I am able to go and come to places on land. Facing the mirror I did not see anything bad in that mirror at that time. Some face see some face cannot see. What does your face see, some are the same thing that I see. Face face when you have sex do you holly because it is good, can you hole sex? Can you stop sex? From coming when the timing is right, no you cannot stop sex your dream will make you have sex. When you have sex with someone you are having time bone. What did you learn from that dream. You know I had talk about to men meeting and, and we did not talk the pump side of me. I am not a pump but I like men. How

can that be, do I need to tell you how can that be. Then if I tell you you will no more than me. Hey this is a joke, let me tell you what I was saying about men. I told a lady once that I like men, and said I did know you was like that, I said, like what, she said funny, I has to laugh at her. Then I said give me your purses, and she said for what, so I, can like them men that you have in your purses she have to laugh, and said everybody like them men. We was talk about money, green. We talk about all thing that unseen and seen, is mud bone some kin to time bone. Where did you find time bone at? Time bone and mud bone is wholing the longest thing you can see of the man body. Who on the right to the bones. The face looking for time bone may never be found. The storm can through the world and stop and start back I seen air break in that storm.

And go to the other place of ress they say. Are you going back to the world when you die Do you really know that, are you just think you know. Do the sleeping dream know. Do you think the devil will every tell the true? Do the devil have a family?

Do you know how old the devil is? Do the day have a mother and father. Do the night have a dad of a mother. Do you think the night and the day or two men. Are do you think they are brother and sister. Did the world have sex, to put all thing in here, we are just think out loud, read along with me. If you have a chance to name the world again what would you name it. But I know this will never happy to a world. If I have a chance to name the world I would name it _____. Do the world o you anything. We are not talking about people in the world that may o you. Do you o the world anything. How many sense do a bull have all of them. This boy though that money was in his pocket, the bull pocket stop bullshitting. A man told me one day if I had to shoe and one sock how many sock would you need, I said one socked he punk me, I said why did you hit, me, he said I got what I need, the other sock. Do the devil every cry. The word hell, I would like to use one letter at a time. H Heaven using e-ever l-lasties l-long did hell ever last long no one never came a said it did. But then, say every lasting. Do you think that we do things to make the world mad. Do the world hole untrue,

maybe people hole untrue, and I think the world also some. How can people lie on people, people tell my age when I was in the month 5 day 20 year 1958 what about when my mother was carrying me for 9 month are whatever the case maybe. We are not changing anything, but I through about when my mother give me a name, are every who gave a name to me. My sis R.L.M if I through about changing my name to Robert love money, but my name is in to the book. We can not get all the thing we like to have. Because I try to have the right to all rights, all my copyright but some was turn around and went to sender. Sent me in the world

And they say, that the idea we sent to be the right of the arena but we was looking for the copyright to the football pool and the right to the basketball pool and the right to all the 200 squares comer block pool. We through that we had one a litter difference from the arena one. We thought we have the pool pool sport room, board game. Do you think this book is instances? We has talk about mom, and what we call her nick names, hear of a few. Nellie Gel Nellie Dim are Nellie bim. At one

time I was think that names was fun, and then I look at it another way. One name was like a light that was dark which one you think will take over the whole world night or day, I do not know, but I hope it never happy. We are face looking. Looking at the ground open up and breath, and eat a lot of thing around the ground. Have you ever seen a man that was born without a nose, and live, he has to breathe out his mouth until the nose is built on to the face, and we know that a dog was born with no ears. No whole just nose eyes face and head; and his body and legs, but no ear. Do you think the dog can hear.

The ground does not have air underground. The ground has to have a nose to get air, unless you dig, a whole to let air in the ground. We did not say anything about water we are talk about the ground. How do we teach a dog that can not hear, you has to show it dog sign, are give it away. The dog born with no ears, can you find out why no ears. We are going to tell you all about West Nile West Nile is a thing that you has to look out for and hope that we can keep safe from the dead of

West Nile. Here are some something to wear, on your head or around your waste are it like a belt, but this belt whole spray that help keep cease the mosquito from biting you. The hat and the shoe that spray deep of off on your body to help safe your life. Vibration or tremor shower brush with water and soap with a towel vibration scratche vibration brush for backs or all over your body. I like to think that I can come up with a idea that will keep you clean every day, the cloth that keep you from stink every day. A new idea we have know put them out yet. The cloth will clean its self, when it clean you, wash and dry on your body. Wear wash and dry cloth automatic wash and dry cloth on your back.

Hey I seen a thing disappear are something evaporate, it's just like someone are in my pocket and my money disappear. Is copper feel in my pocket. The world is just like a evaporate thing come in the world and you and thing disappear, and reappear, some time. When a storm come up on the land is the world sick, do you think the world need a doctor, to help. Do you think the world are weaker are stronger are about the same. Did the

world get wider are long are bigger are small are the same. Did the world made a grade last year. What grade did you give it. I hear nobody gave it a bore. If I had gave it a grade I would have gave it A at because it keep me hear. I like to put light in my eyes, so they can shine like light on a car. My eyes shine in the day time to be able to see day thing. But go black at night, building light in my mind so I can see at night, with only eyes. What does darkness do to people head, or eyes. That is blind in one eyes and can see out the other, are can see out the two light eyes.

Is that the same picture? I said yes, so when I drink the water do I drink the mirror, that are invisible. I talk a little about money, but in my mind I think rich. But I think God for all thing that come in my mind and that come from the mouth of word, the gift of thing to come. I hope that I can handle this knowledge because as I look out in this world I see other trying to handle other their way. New way we handle them so we watch what we do. With the device that will know, keep work with it, and you will know.

If I spell no backward are back and forth n-o

It spell <u>on</u>

Just a through that we recognize and use in my life of living.

The computer smell and tell what you do, any time or some time, are all the time. This computer smell and tell do thing that no one ever know, this device hole all kind of database on so many thing touch taste sight hear and smell, and tell you what you are looking for, in the world. We may not know it all but we are working to be as one that come close to the need of the come of people in all that I can be. Are we can be, to serve and be a man that see something that no other could not find but they are still looking for my stand in the do good work in the place of where I came from. Did I come from smell? I has to go back to smell are back to the place that I came from, no one can get in that space but me. Some people say it about us. I say it about some money also. I like to tell about the water hold my picture, when I look in the ocean and when I look in the mirror I see the picture.

I don't tell my body when it get hunger I know, I

need to feed the body when its hunger. We always has to be repelled back from the power of some or the thing that come from the world. Just say I met a man and reach my hand out to him, to submit his hand. I always say some time, do not hold my hand too long because I am not a pump. Did the world married the earth, who are the male and who is the female, in this case. I am the earth are the world? I am both, because I will always be in the world die are live, are the earth in me. If I had a charge to be in one or the other with one you would come in. We talk about We We one has to be me and the other have to be me, as I live up on this earth I see many thing. Once I was working in the woods and I seen a tree that have leafy that look like a dollar sign $. I call my friend and we talk about that tree for a few minute and then we went back to work. I like to know is we. Safe when we die? From other thing as we leave and repelled back to the (world who or ld) w-or-ld the word spell world but I look at it and I seen something a litter difference. I look at the word (earth) I seen the word here, because it has ear

Different people will have different responses to the book that know, or ask about information that effects my mind, thing natural come and go daily, this book is rich in improves quality of though. You can look further in your thought and you may have something new in you. In your system (I not) hear to judge no one. You are eligible to think for me are for yourself. If you thank for me you have my book, but if you thank for yourself you have your book. This book has to come to the USA some might say this is no good some will say they, that does not know stand we say the book are looking for more books from this book. I say this book will be close, but is not at a crossroad, because it never stop. It just slow down, and wait till it catch up, to the revere one are reveals.

A Picture are a Logo

The circle of eight eyes one eyes is close out, so there will be 7 or seven eyes open in the circle of the eyes.

A picture of the mirror is my reflect of a reflex in the water a picture of to the water and the mirror I put the mirror and the water together, but the water picture will move, so this is the picture that the mirror see. Are this is the picture that water see, so I am drink glass water look like the mirror. Here are the picture of the helmet. The helmet has a pumping hat over the helmet or inside the helmet this is a pump like you use when a baby noise are stop up. Are a hand pump that air go in and out on its own. Its made out of rubber, put, are built the pump and put over helmet. It will stop headlong action try it and see we are try to make the basketball talk and tell who hold the ball too long and who file me. We will built a go bike, we will add a go car to the back of a bike. The half of the go car.

My eyes that shine at night. The eyes light in people eyes that's like you car light. Maybe I cannot put light in my eyes to shine at night but I can put night vision eyes glass. And a house with night vision window, if no one has this window night look like day when you look out your window at night. Can we put night vision glass in car and truck. Hey you need to build a gay bathroom, just look at the business side of it. The USA you have taking some of my word, that I use in my idea are invention. The word SMART, SMART ROBERT

But I am trying to look over that, you using smart in a lot of thing. And I get no money for none of the thing that I put forward. So if you have to tell Jesus something to tell God for you, what will you ask from Jesus. I would ask for one thing, what would that be, you ask for. I see the sun come up in the east and set in the west.

How does the sun go back to the east. Under the world are on top of the world, and be ready to come up in the morning time, are the next day. The sun may come round the side of the world to get back to the east.

When do the USA come clean. You never pay for wrong doing to people that you owe. How can you get away with these people money. Are you a unlawfully country we need to know.

If I ask a lady for her? and she say yes. I look at that as yes spell backward. Sey. But I said who move is it now, one sey my move is hear her move was yes but if she move again before me

This is her on sex

Do you judge wrong answer, you make a lot of error and mistake against us. You just let people man secret get away with without???

I ask white people can you shit white shit they say no, I said why not you shit white shit you are white.

Do people stay mad forever? Why if yes is the way some said how do happiness come in their life.

I try to shit white I eat ice cream and ate white milk white bean I ate white rice. I ate white potato but I did not shit white shit it was yellow brown. I was try to get red white and blue shit, and take picture of this to see how my body color thing.

Sweetro

To my people who like sugar cane syrup the old fashion way, my people use to make the cane in the field, and when it was time to cut the sugar cane down after the planting and the growing of the cane. My grandfather and his family gather the can up and take it to my aunt to make some sugar cane syrup, out of the sugar cane, that came from their fields. So I am trying to learn the business side of the sugarcane making that we are looking to start up again. This is homemade, made with fire and wood are gas to made the sugarcane syrup, if you taste the syrup we make the most natural sugar cane syrup in the world. We mash the juice out the sugarcane and we cook the cane juices for so many hour and then we put the syrup in a jar are some can. For the keeping or the sugar cane syrup we are trying to be a portable sugar cane maker. This is not molasses, this is cane syrup, made outside in the yard.

The face looking company
I remember, it start from this

Look like my eyes and noise of your arm part

What is this a diamond shape
We know what these to is legs

Internet
In her computer I said combooty no it internet,
you better catch him before he fall. Who that man
are that baby

Is there anything call freedom right. For wrong
doer are right for right people you stop stipend

Is you misreprinted

"Read this book, and find out you are writing
your dream! dreamers

People send thing saying you are a winner that
B a lie. You do not win on these letter.

Say I know I can see a stop light in my body. My
shit will give me red and blue, and green, and my
dick give me the flag white and my bobo are dodo

give me the red and blue some time. Do I have to tell you the yellow too, you should know that man. So is this only black booty of mix booty. When I ask that for her and she said yes, and we went to the bed and we will make sex like this, she lay down on the bed on her back, and we are nude then I am get in the bed and I am on my back and we are laying our head is 4 to 5 foot apart and I am putting my dick in her. By get closer to her pussy, put her legs over my legs and I put it in her and play with her per touch lightly and fuck her at the same time for as long as you stay hard in her you can play with her click all that time, you are fuck her. I think I have 7 colors in me that they use in printing.

4 to 5 foot
his hand on her click
me going to her
her coming to you
we on our back

catch me on red app

People Animal and Machine

Hey are Hello

First do not look over this letter, that we are sending to you. My name is Robert Lee Martin and we are looking for some very very good information, from IBM. You built a computer that will smell and tell the doctor about people and touch hear see taste in 5 years sense or smell are in the computer data base or in the cognitive computer search as Waston that is playing and talking on TV. You IBM have to talk to me about my part in the cognitive computer world. I have a provisional application for patent and a non-provisional (utility) patent application filing with and filer authorized by: Attorney Docket Number and name Luca Dotton 2012IDSRM1P power of attorney 56341 we do not no what the power of attorney is up to. He do not get in contact, with us no more, to give us 1 utility provisional patent number to the cognitive computer we are look for IBM to contact us at this phone number 601-807-0628 are sweetro08@ yahoo.com This agreement, dated as of the date

set forth herein, is between IBM non-disclosure and confidentiality agreement This is what we are talk about getting performances contemplated hereby shall be governed and construed under and according to the law of the state of <u>my address</u> 3995 McClain Road Liberty, Miss 39645. Help identify my new smell and tell 1st named Inventor/ Applicant Name: Robert L. Martin

Author: Of Cognitive of thing that tell you about IBM ins 2012???

Hello to Mr. Luca D'Ottone

Robert T. Martin give you the fire going to complement, or the case to see that the non-provisional application, is being forward and true full approval. We thank you for your acknowledgment professional services, and I will wait for the 3-5 years but we hope it can be two years, for the patent numbers. I hope I am not leaving anything out that will slow this work down, you ask for more information my money order gave you the right to go forward. This is a new device no one in my application build the device the right way. The smell and tell device is a thinking and learning device like me. I had build it like a phone boost, to whole data in it, and design studio build for a man to walk through the device, and a talking device that tell thing, to the United State this device whole sense of smell hear touch taste sight or see. I have put all these in a computer, but this is bigger than a computer- by understanding natural language generating hypotheses based on all natural language, relationship between the human and the computer is cognitive technology processes information more like a human than a computer.

This device modified medical center around the world, this is a very important examination for me. I said this device will have banks and all business link to the device. Design studio did not define, but or, part of the device. USPTO will see the need of this invention. This letter is still on the way.

The talking and print out tell and smell device or the printing and talking smell and tell about everything. What every you put this in or on your car truck in your house in your store if they build for all these thing it will know what you did are has not done. This change how people think about what they do. This cognitive computer will make all kind of thing for people to experienced. Individual cooking from this computer will know your dog, cognitive will know you dead or live. Computer smart smell and telling or talking device. I do not know what you all will do with this talking smell and tell device, but it is a different ones from the others. I hope they build to the understand all thing, I do not know that this device need hand and foots are not. To my family Roshana Hou??? and Ladarrius Swan, and my best friend Erica Spe???

These are the people I like for you to contact and carries on if something happen to Robert L. Martin I am looking forward to the non-provisional application patent number are I will sale the patent number when I get it, to the high bid.

This is a man are woman in a device

Narcotic Drug Song Rifa

The legal dope head it all about dope pat head this is yo rap sait it sale on no time to be wrong buy it today sale it to pay by this day dope about dope is here to stay. Roll it blow it light it up and pass the weed. Get your own home grown, get me some. Skins you smoking again. It all about that dope I am going to make you pay for it's all about dope it's a legal feel it how you feeling I am going to make you feel for it growing dope is real this is not a joke this is real smoking dope p dopep dream of some weed 9 foot tall I won't smoke some dope don't want no alcohol dream of a reefer dream of a reefer.

I wake up in morning a half pass ten give me some reefer not no gin dream or a reefer for my I dream or a reefer you smoking dope for this high dream or a reefer can you speak to this high I don't know that I can dream of a reefer I wake up in morning a quarter to five this is legal reefer that no lie dream or a reefer hey look in my eye this is the wee that I try dream or some reefer can I be your supplier smoking on reefer.

Robert keeping my on message

For Copyright connecting my message and data to me and my phone on paper. Instead, I see you talk to the messaging off my phone and from my phone. I hope you can understand what this will tell you about my phone. My phone ideal will do something that phones are not doing now. What I am saying about a phone can scan my paper work from a scanning bar of my messaging that someone sent me this messaging. I can scan this messaging with you scanner and my phone. Can I get paper print off my phone when a messaging that I need when I am in a meeting and you just sent me the messaging I need at that time to close out a deal. I claim the messaging scan bar on and off my phone when you send me a bar scan on my phone or a paper bar on my phone. Paper bar scans you sent. I can use a scanner that they have at their office. They can scan my phone and weigh my truck in and out weighing scale house. Not only scaling truck with my phone but ticket bar codes. This phone can do two things with a messaging

being sent to my phone. Print a paper copy ticket bar codes and scan my phone with your scanning laser scanner to let me in and out office and all other thing with messaging laser.

For copyright connecting date from phone and give it to you on paper Laser, Laser messaging from my phone.

I should say a scanner laser that you can get something off my phone and give this paper off my phone to a company. If I can use the new ideal that can work. Do you have a laser glass or a phone glass that a laser can scan? These laser bar codes can get it off my phone. Not now. But in the time to come, we can see it's coming on your phone. I am not scanning all the things in stores with my phone, but I am trying to scan all the messaging off my phone because I am not always at a computer to download my messages. I need to have hand on this messaging, and I can print if off the phone and scan it with laser and it give me the right paper work and I can turn it in to the company. I am only trying to put more on the phone or messaging getting ticket off my

phone for my work log truck. Putting paper in my phone and being able to pull a piece of paper out my phone with a message on the paper are a laser. Translations from a phone put laser in my phone. I receive a message from my phone. I can pull message from my phone with paper, print out, laser send message on paper off phone paper in phone come out my phone date on to my paper work.

For Copyright connecting Laser Data to and from your Phone

How can I put paper in my phone and get my message in my hand on paper. If I take my phone to any store and message sent to me on my phone, can a store laser scan my phone and tell me what I want to know what is this bar code and how much it cost. I think you can get thing from your Email but I am talking about taking my message from my phone all of my message on my paper from a scan bar laser are paper let do it this way.

| Try to get in moments, | I see and read my message |
| Seconds on paper of my Phone your message on my paper | I need it in my file not left on my phone so you will Have it, I need it. |

This is only to get message from my phone.

My name is Robert Martin

My phone read my last message to me and it tell the phone to print my message on paper or

let it scan bar codes how to get a bar codes for my message that's being sent to my phone.

I see bar codes message talking print out on phone. I need this data on paper. It will never be lost. All data off my phone not lost in my phone just trying to get data in **my** hand on paper. Can I get my paper off the phone with my fingerprint my data on paper out my phone.

Can I take my phone and take a picture of my message and sent the message on my phone to a copy machine.

Robert follows all **my** messages on his entire phone.

Robert wants to change message to another machine or paper come out a phone. Computer smart smell and tell, about me and my book. This it the thinking of the world of the world thinking with people. What are you saying the world book do you have one world book are more, the face looking company what are you saying about the face looking company all people can be a face on your phone to ID. You and it no you just like God

knows you. The whole world gave you the face you have, and it put it together on paper the face looking company, meaning all the people in the world the beginning love walk around the world, so you was in that love walking and riding or setting but you was in the time of day night, I spell my name backward and forward Robert Trebor that was the name and my logo that think like me and is me. I see Watson just like me learning like people. I said my ideal will talk and know thing that in the world. Computer Smart Smell and tell your doctor when the doctor tells you to blow in my Computer Smart Smell and tell our sickness by your breath in the phone. This book open up more new world that I can put together. Some people will try to separate day night. They will say day are night but we say day night. How will I believe top spell top and backward. It spell pot. Do a pot hold the world up? If I say top air ground, is that all the world? I said no you have pot. All are you are in my company. I am talking about people are machine that in my company when the moon come out you will call that night light. The world hold you in his arms are her arms this book think it no,

god wife hold you in her arms. Where she at? In the face looking company, everything have a face. Do it? I said god has a wife, because other people could not say it. So I had to tell the work to get it off my mind. Reading myself as my time to though the world. I look at myself and I cannot see my face but that does not mean that I am dead. That is a dead spot that you cannot see in the ground, but you in a mirror, you can see your life in that mirror. So it takes to see one. Was that three me in the mirror and my picture. So it take two to see three. No it take three to see one face me in the mirror and the picture, you tell me. A mirror hold the true picture of me. I think that is the way god see me on earth. You tell me. You probable can speak one world twice at a time. What is it that I tell on paper a way to read and know about things that no one have a thought but you. You do have a thought or an opinion on walking and stopping in your life. I have to stop reading the world mine. If I keep going I will have been around the world. So it can tell me some good just like it taste good. I can see good come from the ground. I said I had seen her in my writing did you come close enough

to see her for yourself so yourself is your identity and then you will discover thing to be done. Do you think the cross has four feel it. Why did you say that. Because a bird talk you talk a man talk and a computer talk. I had said you cannot speak to word at one time. If you do you will be doubled mined and doubled mouth. Put my smart back in my computer. Smart Smell and Tell. Why did you take my smart and try to use if for our ideal that you need to return it to me and or pay me for it. How can you take someone work from them. This is one I copyright that I have the copy number.

Two who, is there to dog to God to who know I am writing this book to the one that understand what I am saying in or out the world of thinking with sense to do thing in the mind and then build this or put it together. Together is that together like my mine think how to put two things in one place. Together mean you are here with me. Think that I can see in my mind but not in the world of mine. One day night somebody will see what I has said if you does not see it now. Looking is a great way move more easily when looking for someone or thing. Did you see her? I say top air ground pot top is god you tell me the rest. When you come into the world, some love you and we can see love the way it grow around the world. Are you in the writing? Start when the beginning was but start the N the N is hear. In my mine is there a in sense in my brain of in my mine with one hold sense is to N of a begin a N. I god. I being. I wife or my wife. I message. I world. I universe. I no. I identity. I discover. Man you are a man, yes because you smell like a man because you are a funky mother fucker. I start and I stop. I open, I way. I face new air new day new night.

Looking I smart way

Writing my own knowledge. Things I see. Cricket is a tree. Grow cricket lightening did the day come in straight or night came in straight. How can you measure it? The reason I said that because lightening when it lightning hard it moves something. Day night do the sun has anything to do with daylight? Day night can be separation from the world. I am in a computer machine world that has a sense with me in. Not the earth computer I am talking about the world how it work. I like to patent Robert Lee Martin and all of my knowledge. Do God has or have an in sense to discover and create. They say patent pending for me to be in computer-Smart Smell and Tell. My picture, my whole body and message. My knowledge for words for me myself only. One day became night but I did not see night become day. I saw moonlight but not night day. I saw day become night for some hour. Do the wife has are have a sense are in sense to create and discover. Maybe you come close to measure the change by time. I will read my book when it come out in the earth of people. No I am not talking about my book is coming out are people when you read it I will read it then I know it's on

the world mind. I got mine obtained and trying to recovered all of it. I am I. In the begin thank to the names family that no me and all my friends. This is not talking about no one in particular every are so smart in their own way. I try to find the smart in dome. Is dome smart is smart dome. I hear people say you over grown. When you are not over grown at what age are over grown are there an un grown. To me when I get overgrown next thing I am dead or what.

Patent pending me in heaven.

What pen me in hell. Not now what you do to stop from to that place. Can you see the sun hide from the night. The sun that comes out in the daytime does not come out at night. I never saw that before in my life. All thing of patent on earth are number seen like the world no everything about me and you. Have you ever hide from the world. How can you do that. I people can hide from people in the world do not try to hide from the world because I see you. I all way see the moon come around in the daytime at night anytime. I will all way say you cannot separate something. Time will not come apart. I did not say stop time. I said pull it in half. The only way you can pull your time in half. I will leave you and my time pull away from you but the world time will not do it like that. Thank to all the people that doctor on me all the time when I was sick, you help me and thank again. But for me to write this I feel this book out and all thing that came with my being on the earth and I put these thing in the world of you can learn and see people want to judge people. You cannot make it work.

The world will have a true device and will write your right and wrong smart world smart court room build it. It will no you and what you do to be judged and it will not let you get away and hide behind other people building true to stop lie that people put on other people. I thought God people was put on the world to live the true. I see machine live true.

Separate dialogue opportunities.

Undome oven smart. I am oven smart. You will learn more about me by reading my tag on my car. My tag will have all my license and my address. The tag holder will give this to the police when you pull behind me. The police can know my name. My license number. If I do something or break the law. You can write me a ticket off my car and mail it to my phone number that the tag holds all the things that the law needs. And I do not have to stop on the side of the road. You need to change in this world to an electronic tag on my car only for the police use and keep me safe. The police will have a device in front of his car when he get behind me he can turn his to see my information on line. I will not give police everything about me just something. This is not a test to read this book. This is a book to post all to your friend and see what can they get out of the mind of knowledge. I cannot say that you understand of your knowledge. Learning my machines no knowledge and it my time. Keep to God knowledge. I sign in time I see knowledge. I

hear knowledge. I understand. Do you hear good? My voice representative, my petition to revive.

I sign in time	Look Time I Keep
Oven Smart	Smart I way